OMC

C000056542

My mother was right!

By

Fiona Stöber

Inspired
by
Patricia Mary Bernadette Haylock

Better known
as
"Mam"

OMG

MY MOTHER WAS RIGHT!

Part of the profits earned by this book will be donated to the various charities my dear Mam supported so passionately her whole life.

"Look to the future with hope and optimism,
It is faith and belief that will help you move mountains.
You will never be alone if you believe I am still close,
Life is for living, be sure to enjoy it"

Patricia Mary Bernadette Haylock

For Pat

My angel without wings

Contents

- If you are a Duchess, then be a Duchess
- It is a shame to be shabby
- Bless them and send them on their way
- Inferiority is easily overcome – use superiority- make people feel good it´s contagious
- It is how you feel that matters
- If you say you can you can, if you say you can´t you can´t!
- If you ask the question, listen to the answer
- Life is cruel for taking away our loved ones, but kind for giving them to us in the first place
- Don´t hate just intensely dislike
- If you fall in shit, make sure you come out smelling of roses
- Happiness is an inside job

To sum it up!

Who was Pat?

A forever note for my Mam

You are my inspiration to be the very best version of "me" I can possibly be. You continue to teach me every single day.

With all my heart, I thank you for being a more priceless gift than words can express. In eternal gratitude for a bond that will never break, thank you for being my Mam.

Acknowledgements

Thank you to everyone who helped me, supported me and guided me through the last 2 years. Special thanks go to Leona for the wonderful illustration, you are a true talent, thank you so much. A cloud full of glitter has to be thrown over my family for their never-ending support, love and encouragement and for their inspiration while sharing their own stories of my Mam's encouragement. The biggest word of thanks goes to my Mam, wherever you are, you were so right.

Thanks

Introduction

8.30 am

"Hiya mam it's just me!"

"Hiya Pet, I was just thinking about you, I'm busy saying my prayers and thanking God for you and your lovely family. I am so excited I'm going see you tomorrow. We're going to have such a lovely time, I've got the present wrapped and it's in my handbag so it doesn't get lost. I've got one for "littly" (the nickname Mam gave to my son) too. Hers (my daughter) is as precious as she is and his is very special just like him, just in case I don't make it to his 18th."

"Mam!" I snapped "Don't say that!" she continued:

"You never know pet (this is a word we use in Geordie our dialect for darling, treasure or sweetheart) you never know the moment. Fi, who would have thought 18 years ago, remember that was when I fell and broke my knee cap and I couldn't get to you when she was born. Well I've made up for it, I have never missed a birthday since."

"You're the best Mam, my angel without wings, it's no wonder he answers your prayers!"

"He answers my prayers because I always say thank you darling, you must always remember to say thank you, it doesn't matter how hard times get sweetheart, always look for the good, you will always have a reason to be grateful and that will help change things for the better.

"God Mam, you are so wise, where would I be without you? Remember last year when you surprised her, she nearly fell down the stairs when she saw you standing there, I will never forget that moment, neither will she."

"Me neither, there was no way I was missing a birthday, we're so lucky Fi, so lucky to have this bond and I will be with you tomorrow."

"Right up you get and get that case packed, I am off to the shops and getting your room ready. Speak to you later."

"OK, love you millions and see you tomorrow."

"love you more"

And off I went in my whirlwind life getting everything ready for what was going to be the best 18th birthday we could possibly give our little girl. Well, she wasn't very little anymore, she is taller than me! All the same she never ever wanted to grow up and Mam and I laughed regularly about it and so we promised when she got to 18 we would make it worth it for her to be an adult.

The cake was ordered, the balloons and streamers were in Grandma's case, the Moet was already chilling, the surprise guests were all informed and the party could begin.

OMG what about a cake to celebrate her birthday in, we need sparklers for that.

10.20 am

"Mam it´s me, where are you? Give me a ring back as soon as you get in, I need you to pop to the shops and get me something, we´re making an amazing cake for midnight, I need your help! Love you…see you tomorrow!"

The excitement in my voice was now more than evident. I loved my Mam more than any words could say or any number could quantify. I have adored her since the day I was born. To be honest we are so similar sometimes I question whether we both came out of the same egg only at different times, but that would be silly so I will just leave it at the fact that I love every bone in her body and I absolutely idolize her. She can do no wrong, not for me, don´t get me wrong she does wrong like all of us, big time wrong sometimes and it normally involved Gin, but I don´t care, it´s never enough to push her off the pedestal I have her on.

10.45 am

"Hiya love, it´s just me, I was out with the boy (her dog). He´s going on his holidays this afternoon so we were just having a lovely last walk."

"Hiya, bless him. He doesn´t care, he loves going to Carols, I hope Beth is there for him, he´ll be delighted."

"He's a cheeky thing, he doesn't even look back when he gets out of the car. No doubt Carol will have stocked up on the treats for him. I am so lucky she has him. He loves her."

"Mam are you going shopping?"

"I knew you would need something last minute, what do you want? I wasn't going but I can do."

"We're making this chocolate cake and when you open it, Maltesers fall out, it's lush she is going to love it, but I need Maltesers and loads of them!"

"We? who's the royal we?" Laughing as always Mam answered

"I'll pop up when I drop the boy off, anything else?"

"No, that's it. I have got everything. I am so excited Mam she is going to have such a lovely birthday"

"I know, I can't wait, I am painting my nails gold so that I am modern, I hope I have got the right things to wear, there is no room in my suitcase it's full of streamers, plastic cups and balloons!"

"Don't worry we'll have plenty of time to shop!"

"I can't wait love, see you tomorrow. Love you!"

"Love you more"

15.20 pm

"Hiya love it´s me!"

"Hiya, I am running around like I am preparing the royal wedding!"

"Slow down, I will be there tomorrow to help you. Don´t do your ironing, I´ll do that after the party."

"Thanks Mam, I will have to do some, there is loads."

"You little monkey, you say that every time. Well, I´ve got 5 big packets of Maltesers and the case is closed. I am just going to clean my fridge and make my tea and then I´ll give your Aunty Judy a call and then I am having an early night."

"You always do that, you always go to bed early so the next day comes quicker.!"

"I know. Anyway, you go and get on and I will see you tomorrow."

"Love you. See you tomorrow!"

"Love you too treasure!"

18.50pm

"Just quick it´s me!"

"Hi pet, what do you need?"

"Nothing what time is your flight in do you know?"

"It's BA I think it's the 6 'o clock, don't worry if you get stuck in traffic, I will just wait."

"No, I will be there. Love you"

"Love you too, see you tomorrow and we'll have a big cuddle!"

"I can't wait, Mam I am so excited. The kids are popping, even Molly knows you are coming"

"Love you"
"Love you more"

<u>Tuesday 6th March</u>

7.45 am

"Hiya Mam it's just me, you must be in the bath. I will call again later to make sure you are up. See you later, love you!"

9.45 am

"Hiya it's me. You must have left already. I will try your mobile!"

11.25 am

"Hiya Mam, I still can't get you. You must be getting your "meal deal" in Boots. Give me a ring back when you get to Heathrow. Have a good flight. Love you. See you later….can't wait…love you!"

14.35 pm

"It's just me again. I hope you haven't forgotten your phone, give me a call back to let me know you are ok. Love you!"

15.15 pm

"This is strange, you must be boarding. Hope all is on time. Love you. See you soon. Love you.!"

15.20 pm

"Stu (my brother), have you spoken to Mam today?"
"No why? Have you not either? I sent her a text at 7.30 but she hasn't replied. I just thought she must be busy! What time is she due in?"

"6, she is probably already on the plane and she will have her phone off. I have been running around I must have missed her!"

"Ok, let me know when she arrives. Give me a ring straight away.!"

"Will do brother, love you."

"Love you too"

What happened next was going to change my life forever. If somebody had told me what was going to happen in the following few hours, days and weeks, I would have said there was no way on earth I could cope with it. I know a lot of people have to feel pain in this life, and I also know that my pain was no worse than anyone else´s. However, one fact remains, something that I was unaware of at the time, something that has fascinated me ever since especially when reflecting back on those unbearable days and weeks. The moment grief struck was the moment I subconsciously knew that I was prepared to cope with whatever life was about to throw at me because this amazing teacher I was so privileged to be able to call my Mam, had taught me some basic mindsets, knowingly or unknowingly, but I was prepared to cope with what life was about to throw my way.

This book shares with you some basic truths my Mam taught me. We laughed at her, we often didn´t listen, we sometimes said "thank you" and sometimes we didn´t. She didn´t care.

She lived by some very wise principles that she shared with us all and I mean us all, her friends, her family, her colleagues, people she met walking the dog, people she met in the street, shopping or on holiday, Mam didn´t care who you were. What she did care about was sharing her wisdom and she did it on a daily basis.

These principles have helped me remain sane in a time I can only describe as the hardest and darkest days of my life. The pain has numbed me, the loss has left me staring into thin air but still her words, wise as they are, ring daily in my ears helping me to come to terms with my new "now" and helping me to find light in what seemed darker than darkness. Her words have become glitter and as I hold onto every single thing she taught me, I am starting to feel better and now looking back in amazement that I got through that awful time in my life I have to say:

O_h M_y G_{od...}

My Mother was right!

Foreword

The traffic had been horrendous. There was something in me that had known since this morning that something wasn´t right. I talked to my Mam every single day on the phone, often 2 & 3 times. Today of all days we would have talked constantly, we were so excited. Yet I hadn´t heard a word. I must have called her phone 20 times as I was approaching the airport, strangely it was still ringing. I convinced myself she hadn´t switched it onto airplane modus and instead she had just switched the ringer off. Inside I knew differently, I knew something had gone wrong.

I drove into the airport and parked directly in front of the terminal. I ran into the arrivals hall and looked at the board. The Heathrow flight had landed already, it was early, I breathed a sigh of relief, silly me, worrying about nothing that's why the phone had rung, they had landed already.

I stood amongst the crowd of happy people, some with balloons, others with flowers, a lady with her dog stood next to me and smiled.

"You look excited!" she said to me.
I smiled back

"My Mam is coming from England, it´s my daughters 18th birthday, she has never missed a single one, she has been to every birthday!"

"Oh, wow lucky you, have a wonderful time. I am waiting for my Son, he lives in London!"

I was relieved they weren´t out yet. Just then her son came out of the doors.

"Have a wonderful time!"
"Thanks, you too!"

I waited.

18.10 pm

"Stu it´s me, she´s not here!"

"What do you mean, when should she have arrived, are you sure? Stay where you are, I will call you back."

My brothers voice remained calm, mine however started to panic.

I ran out of the Arrivals Hall 2 to the Arrivals Hall 1 in the next terminal, perhaps I had got the terminal wrong.

There she was, OMG the relief in my body.

"Mam, thank god, I thought you hadn´t arrived! Sorry I was at the wrong terminal!"

The lady turned around......... it wasn´t my Mam!

I fell to my knees.

Please God, this cannot be happening to me, not this week please, not me.

Her words already ringing in my ears:

"Why not you?
why not this week?"

No Mam please!

My phone rang.

"Fi, get back in your car, she's not coming. Her passport hasn't been used. There is an emergency team on its way to her house!"

I froze.

"Stuart, how do you know? Are you sure?" my voice was starting to break, my brother was calm and assertive, firmly he replied

"I know Fi, get back in your car. I am on my way to Newcastle."

I called my sister, she was already on her way to Newcastle too.

Mum had suffered a Traumatic Brain Injury falling down her stairs, we do not know how long she had been there but she was still alive when the emergency services got to her. She cardiac arrested twice, had an emergency operation to cut open her skull and free her brain from the pressure and she was put on life support.

I prayed as hard as I could for a miracle. The miracle I was granted, was that I had 5 weeks to sit next to my Mams bedside holding her hand and massaging her feet with Chanel cream to keep her like the princess I had always held her for. She fought like a trojan, and against all odds she actually regained consciousness to a level that we found a way to communicate, it was amazing. Her sheer determination and belief and of course the amazing ICU care she was given from the R.V.I hospital in Newcastle Upon Tyne, gave us time to get used to the fact that she was leaving us.

After 5 weeks she smiled, closed her eyes and walked to the other side of the rainbow.

Her wisdom and her love, her optimism and her amazing ability to make every person she touched feel at ease, lives on in her wise words.

These are the words I feel compelled to share with you all in this book.

In memory of one of the nicest people I have ever known, and I was lucky enough to call her "Mam."

I hope you find some glitter in her words that may help to allow your life to shine brightly.

Enjoy!

Be Kind or Don´t Be!

My Mam was one of the kindest people I have ever known (The other one I was lucky enough to marry.) This is not my own biased opinion if you asked anyone to describe her, the first thing people would say was that she was kind, followed by what a lovely smile she had.

Mam always said that is was important to be kind. She told us if we couldn't be kind then we should better not do what we were doing. Suddenly kindness takes on a whole new life. It depends on how you see life, kindness isn't always just an action, kindness can be words, thoughts, gestures, body language, reactions, thoughts. Kindness normally results in putting a smile on someone else's face, that's when you know you have been kind. You may not always see the smile and you most certainly also sometimes do acts of kindness for your own gain, this is fine too. However, most of the time you may not even know how kind you have been to someone, it's the way the other person receives your gesture that decides whether or not it is kind and not what you put out there.

The best thing we can do is simply try always to be empathetic towards others, do as you like to be done to yourself and then you can rest assured that you are giving your best and being as kind as you possibly can be.

My Mam always said:

"If you have the choice,
do the nice thing, be kind!"

Kindness will come flowing back to you in many different ways.

Sometimes it is not easy to be kind because actually we don't think the person on the receiving end of our kindness deserves it. Mam always said that it is in times when we really have to try hard to be kind, that it's really worth the effort. This is because, it is then that we ourselves will feel so much better, when we're in a situation of struggle, and we take the time to stop and do something kind.

Actually, when we feel good, life is always good back to us. Not necessarily from the person we were kind to, often from somewhere completely different but it always reflects back to us.

Being kind to yourself is also very important. If you are kind to yourself you will find it is much easier to be kind to others because you will feel inner contentment. It is not selfish to be kind to yourself on the contrary, you are of much more use to others and much more inspiring for others when you have inner contentment.

It is also very important to remember that kindness isn't always just an action. Kind thoughts are as equally, sometimes more, important than actions. Often, we get ourselves annoyed about a situation, sometimes something that has happened at work or in a relationship, sometimes a simple thing like someone annoying us while we're driving. In such situations we always have a choice, we can get ourselves upset and have annoying thoughts about that person or the situation. Or, we can, as my Mam used to say "Bless them and send then on their way!" in other words: have a kind thought and let the situation go.

So, the advice is simple. If you have the choice and one of those is to be kind, BE KIND. It is always worth it.

Be true to yourself, give as much as you possibly can every day and make a difference!

"There is no point trying to be anyone other than yourself, you will never manage that!"

I heard this saying so often while I was growing up.
Mam used to say:

"You are the best and only person capable of being you, so enjoy the journey!"

It is so true! We always want what we cannot have. There is absolutely nothing the matter with wanting, that is healthy it helps us strive to achieve every day. In fact, my dear Dad used to say to my Mam:

"Can you not stop wanting?"

She would answer:

"The day I stop wanting, you start worrying!"

There was a lot of truth in those words. It is healthy to want but you have to know what you want and who you want to be. It is no use wanting to be someone else because you will never ever achieve this. We are all unique and wonderful individuals and the more we stay true to our own selves the happier our lives will be.

There is an instinct in all of us. My Mam used to call it our warning signal, it is your gut feeling and it never ever lets you down. It will always tell you if you are on the right track to be you. If it feels right, it is right and if it feels wrong it probably is. There is a talent in distinguishing between feeling wrong and being afraid, this is covered in another saying.

Basically, if you live your life true to "yourself" and you are kind to yourself and others around, you will regularly see that you can make a difference to the world you are living in. These differences will be slight and subtle but they will "be" and that is what counts.

It is a really satisfying feeling to feel contentment and satisfaction because you have given your best to the day and made a positive difference to those you have shared it with.

Mam encouraged me to give as much as I possibly could every day, to simply be the best "me" I could be and to try my best to make a positive difference to everything that came my way, she encouraged me to make this my priority every day.

Thanks, you were right again. The feeling is awesome!

Your goal must be "JOY!"

Joy is definitely one of the most satisfying emotions. It is what we enjoy as much in giving it, as we do in receiving it. There are many different things that give us joy and often the things that give one person joy may not necessarily be that same thing that gives someone else joy.

It is everyone's own awareness of a situation that allows it to be joyful for one and not for the other. However, one thing is for certain, we all love the feeling when we find joy. If you can feel pure joy, you will feel contentment and that is ultimately one of our inner goals.

Some people find it in music, others in books through words, others in prayer and others still in sharing time with certain people like family and friends. The most important thing is that you keep aiming for it. Often the journey of looking for joy can bring as much joy as in finding it. The more joy you see and feel, the more you will experience on the way. Because you don't know what other people are perceiving at any one time so all you can do is concentrate on your own perception and make the most of it by looking for the joy that suits you. The benefit of this is that you feel better. It doesn't mean you end up in another place, or even in a better place because when you feel joy it doesn't matter where you are, all that matters is that you feel joyful. Because that is a great place to be.

Children and animals are our best teachers of reminding us of how good feeling joy actually is. Children feel joy in small things and they delight in the fun that they have whilst discovering it. Animals rarely allow others to influence their feeling of joy and bliss. A cat can lie for hours in the sun, purring in joy because of the joy the sun rays are giving it, the cat doesn't get distracted by the lawn mower or the traffic passing by or or or. The cat concentrates solely on the joy it is feeling in the moment.

Mam often told me when I was frustrated and unhappy with a situation to look for joy both in the journey and in the goal. She always said it is in joy that I will find satisfaction. In the end we are all just trying to move away from pain, it is that simple.

So, she would say:

"If you aim anywhere,
aim for joy,
feel it for the moment
and enjoy it
while it lasts!"

"You"
can´t make a wrong decision

The older I get, the more this makes sense to me. When I was younger, I never quite understood how my Mam could tell me off for doing something wrong and then 10 minutes later, tell me I couldn´t make a wrong decision as whatever I do, whichever way I choose to go, it´s my journey and every road leads me, to where I am going. She always added:

*"If it is meant for you,
it won´t pass you by!"*.

So how is it, that we can´t get it wrong? Well according to my dear Mam, everything we do is always part of our journey. So have no regrets! There is no such thing as wrong it is just someone else´s perception. If you have done it and you think it is right and your heart and soul is in it, then it is right for you. Someone else´s perception may however think it is wrong, that´s where the problem lies, in how much you care what others think and how much you allow that to influence you. Of course, there are laws we have to keep to, I am talking about making everyday decisions that are sometimes hard. Also remember this advice works in both ways, sometimes we think people are wrong and if we dare to see it through their eyes, we may see a different picture. YOU have to be non-judgemental

Whatever decisions you make, as long as they feel truly right for you, then they will be. Sometimes we feel obliged to make our decisions based on a million other factors like what other people think of us, who the decision will affect and how the outcome will change everything. This is the hard part of this advice, you have to initially make the decision to suit yourself, then weigh up whether it is worth it (for you and only for you!) or if you would make the decision differently because actually the outcome is not actually what you want after all.

Sometimes however, and this is true to the things that really are meant for us in life, you just know deep inside of yourself that the decision is the right one. The problem is that it is hard to make because you know you are going to upset others around you by making it, this is when you really have to be true to your gut feeling and do what feels best for you. Sometimes we still choose another path than the one we want to take and this is ok too. This is when the saying really supports you:

"**You** can't get it wrong!"

You see life is good to us, if something is meant for you, it will turn up in your life so often and in so many different ways, until you accept it. So next time you are struggling to make a decision, make it to suit how you feel at that moment in time, be true to yourself and know that you can't get it wrong, because if life wants you to have or experience something else, it will appear in your future again quicker than you know!

If you believe strongly in something, then make the decision and follow the path it will take you on. If you believe it is right for you, then there is an experience to be had in it and you can't get it wrong.

Everyone needs a passion

My Mam epitomized this in so many ways. She had a handful of passions and she was truly focused on every one of them. What she didn't tell me, but what I have learnt going through life, is that as we go through life, we have a number of passions, all equally as important as the last one but they appear at different times in our lives and sometime they are only important for a small time, others stay with us for a life time.

To have a passion, means that you want to put your body and soul into something because you believe in it or in someone so much. It is truly a very satisfying feeling knowing that you have a passion. It makes the day easier to get through when it's hard, it makes life easier because if you have a passion, you have a purpose and if you have a purpose you have a goal and if you have a goal you will feel a sense of achievement and if you feel achievement you will experience JOY and joy in my Mams eyes, is what we should all be aiming for.

The importance in this message lies in the emphasis that we have a passion. There is such a huge difference if we do something whatever it may be, with a passion or not, the results say it all.

Take for example gardening. I don't really get a lot of joy from gardening at this moment in time in my life. I do it because I like a nice garden and I thoroughly enjoy sitting in my garden when it's all done and it gives me great pleasure. My sister on the other hand is passionate about her garden and she doesn't just get pleasure from the finished product on the contrary I think she never sees her garden as "finished," it is an on-going project. However, if her and I did the same garden hers would feel so much more beautiful than mine when it is finished because she works in it with passion, I work in mine with the hope that I am finished soon so I can sit and enjoy it. She finds the enjoyment in simply being in her garden, whatever she is doing.

Another example is sport, if you play tennis against someone who is passionate about the sport, their game will be a completely different one as opposed to playing against someone who is just playing for the hell of it.

The best example is music, listening to someone who is passionate about what they are playing sounds completely different to someone who is just playing the instrument.

Mam always said if you can find your passion and work with it, your work will always glow, you have to find a passion because it feeds your soul. It doesn't matter what it is, it is YOUR passion and it doesn't have to feel magical to anyone but you, however if it's a true passion, others will feel the magic through you.

Mam did almost everything she did from being a Mam, to playing sport even doing her crafts and speaking to people, she did it all with a passion, I guess that's why she has left such an amazing impression on so many people.

Don't be afraid to love your passion, and let it change as often as you want, but make sure you act passionately about things that mean a lot to you. It's good for your soul my Mam would say ☺

My favorite taste is
"bitter-sweet"

For those of you who knew my Mam I can hear you laughing already, she was a great lover of a G&T, the bitterness of the gin and the sweetness of the tonic, but there was a lot more truth to this saying than I ever consciously understood until she passed away. The bitter sweet she really loved was always experiencing both sides of life, and god knows she had her fair share of both sides of the coin. She would say when she was in the depths of hard times, when you hit the gutter the only way is up and that's a magical journey.

"when you are in the gutter
the only place left to go
is the sewer
and when you get there
the only way
is back up!"

She always said you can't have the light without the dark, the sweet without the sour, the rough without the smooth, the good without the bad. It isn't until you actually experience something on the bad side that you really appreciate and consciously enjoy how good the good side can be. So next time you find yourself in a situation that is bad and not good, sour instead of sweet, hard instead of easy, stop and think.

Because you now know this, you also know how wonderful the opposite is, how great the good is, how fulfilling light is, how perfect peace is. When you then exert gratitude for the wonderfulness that life is offering you, even the smallest of things amidst the hard times and there Is always a ray of light to be found, it is the universal law. There always has to be a positive with every negative, we sometimes just have to look really hard to find it. So, every time you think how bad or hard times are, stop that thought and immediately look for one simple thing that's good, it may be a smile a stranger offers you at the bus stop, or the warmth of the sun, it may be the happy love your pet offers you or a kind gesture your colleague does for you because you are having a bad day. Hold on to that positive and be grateful for it and very quickly the sweetness of life will return to you and before you know it the negative things become less and less. The secret here is really to always look for the positive in things even if they really don't look like there is anything positive in it.

She would say:

"Remember love, you can only appreciate the sweetness if you have tasted the sour!"

That doesn't mean you have to hang around and only have the sour, just a quick taste is enough, but I will guarantee you that the sweet will taste much so much better after it!

Have you ever done a spa and after the sauna gone in the cold water, the warmth afterwards feels so much better than if you don't go in the cold.

So, Mams favorite taste being bitter sweet meant she was in the middle. She used to say the best taste is bitter sweet because if you are in the middle you can enjoy everything. Sometimes we go to extreme, when its good we love it, but when its dark we don't and that's when you have to take charge of your mind and start looking for the good to be grateful. But how do we know what the extreme of light is if we have never felt the extreme dark? I can tell you losing my Mam in the way she left this earth took me to the darkest place ever, even though I had lost my dear father just 2 years prior to losing my Mam. Loosing Dad was dark, god it was awful, but I was prepared, he had cancer and so even before he left us and I felt that emptiness death so cruelly offers, I was already starting the process of gratitude by telling myself it was better for him as he didn't have to suffer anymore. In reality, Mother Nature, had instinctively already started the same process my Mam had shared with me in her bitter/sweet stories. However, when Mam left this earth, her accident tore me out of my "light" reality into a new "dark" reality with no warning, no preparation and no immediate obvious way through it. It was hard, believe me, it was dark, really dark in fact I think that was to date my darkest experience and it didn't taste good. I got myself out of that by exerting gratitude, by constantly reminding myself of the good times we had, of the fun we had, the love we shared of the sweet that we were so lucky to be allowed to taste so very often. I must add here, much more than we ever tasted sour and because of that now when I look back, I can smile at the sour and then I embrace the sweet because it's the combination, the bitter sweet that tastes so good. I was so grateful for this advice, the pain was so hard of not having her physically close, some days it quite literally took my breath away, and to be honest it still does, the shock, the sadness, the pain, the darkness of this experience in my life hasn't gone away, I don't suppose it ever will, but I have learnt to live with it by covering it in what I call "grateful glitter".

I throw "grateful glitter" everywhere I feel negativity and that helps me to start to feel better and slowly emerge from the darkness back into the light and to live with the taste of "bitter sweet life."

"It doesn't matter how hard times get sweetheart,
always look for the good,
you always have a reason to be grateful and that
will help change things for the better"

What is Grateful Glitter?

Grateful glitter is an expression Mam and I used to throw on situations that didn't make us happy, basically sad moments. This does not mean we didn't feel sadness, we did, but we didn't hang around it too long to let it start eating away at us. We would accept it, have a cry and a cuddle and then start thinking of reasons we were grateful for the situations. Also, people, if people were annoying us or behaving in a different way to the way we wished they were towards us, instead of getting annoyed or hurt or upset, we would throw "grateful glitter" at it and find reasons to be grateful for the lessons we were learning, the new side of people we were seeing etc. It didn't mean we accepted it, we just changed our way of looking at it to make it more bearable for us.

The saying "grateful glitter" originally came from my Grandad. He used to call me "Funnyona" (funny and Fiona ☺) because when I was poorly or I had hurt myself or I was upset about something, he used to call me "Funnyona" to make me laugh. As I got older and he got poorly, I used to sit and play dominos with him and try to make him laugh or tell him all reasons I was grateful for him and my little Nana. One day he said to me "there she goes, "Funnyona" spreading her grateful glitter and making me happy!"

From then onwards, Mam and I used to throw "grateful glitter" at things we wanted to cheer up.

Two wrongs do not make a right

I love this one and I bet you have all heard it a million times growing up.

It is so true and although it annoyed me while I was bickering with my brother and sister as we were growing up, it has been a very important piece of advice in my adult years.

Two wrongs really do not make it right. So next time you are determined to prove your point and show someone that they have done you wrong, think twice. If you can do this without doing wrong yourself, ok. However, if it involves doing wrong to prove your point, think twice. "Be bigger than that" my Mam would say and do not lower yourself down to someone else´s level to prove your point.

You can make it right by accepting someone else´s point of view, this does not mean you agree with them in any way, it means you agree to disagree.

*Never,
lower your moral high ground
for the sake of
proving a point!*

End something
when it´s at its best,
don´t wait for it to turn

This saying actually helped me in my darkest moments just after my Mam passed away. We were all very upset and to be honest in a state of disbelief that she had actually left us, suddenly my daughter started to laugh, I asked her what she was laughing about and she said:

"Oh Mummy, typical of Grandma, I just had a funny thought. I just thought to myself, if Grandma was here, she would say to us, "Sorry I have to get out of here, I have seen the best there was, I am not waiting for it to turn, I don´t want to get old!". My daughter said: "You know mummy, if she had survived her brain injury her life would never have been the same, it wouldn´t have been as good, she knew she had seen the best and true to her word she was gone!"

The tears were streaming down my face but I knew she was right.

This was a very sad example but what Mam taught me was to always be aware of the situation you are in. You have to feel your way through things and know when you have had the best of it and when you have given all you can to it. Then it makes sense to leave while the going is good.

You are not stuck because you can´t,
you are stuck
because you won´t

*"There is nothing wrong with not succeeding,
but there is so much wrong
with not trying"*

Her words are still very vivid every time I try something new. I even hear myself saying her exact words to my own kids. She always encouraged us to try everything. She believed if we wanted something, we could have it and that there was no such word as "can't".

However, she was not shy of hard work. She also believed that if you were not getting what you wanted then you needed to either change your strategy or put more work into it. This is where the "won't" in her quotation comes from. She basically taught us that if we found ourselves in a position where we really believed we could not go any further, and we wanted to (this is crucial!) then we had to change something to make it happen. If we stayed stuck in the same place saying "I can't" she would say "Yes you can, you won't". What she meant was, if you want it that much you have to change and you have to want that otherwise you won't move forward.

My Mam was a great believer in hard work. She was an avid sportswoman and she knew what it meant to put the work in, she also said "it's not enough to do it, you have to make sure you do it properly!"

"If you say you can you can, if you say you can't you can't!"

I have cursed at these words so many times in my life that I have lost count how many times it was. Growing up I was always a very inquisitive, alert little girl but there was one thing I always relied on knowing that I was confident simply knowing my Mam was always behind me.

My Mam was so focused. If she wanted something, she went for it and she focused on it to a point, that it actually sometimes got annoying (I guess this is a character thing ☺.) If she wanted you to do something then she wanted you to do it now, she didn't want you to do it tomorrow or next week, she would ask you if you could help and then she would expect you to give your all.

Mam would write a list, know her goal, devise a strategy, get her team in place and not give up until she got to where she wanted to be.

Today, if I find myself in a situation where I feel I am not getting to where I want to be, I stop and ask myself "where did I lose focus?" Then, I simply realign myself and carry on.

She wouldn't care if she failed to get exactly what she set out for. Mam was flexible in her expectations of herself and of others, and I guess this was the secret to the success. She always said you are better to have tried and failed or even only half achieved than never to have tried at all, that way you have achieved what you could.

She would always ask if we had given our best, she never waited for the answer, she told us to answer that ourselves, after all she truly believed we ourselves were our own benchmark, our only true competition. The greatest day is the one that ends in you saying "I did my best today!"

In my Mam's eyes if you did your best, you achieved.

If you can´t say anything good then don´t say anything at all!

We all love a little gossip about people and situations and there is nothing wrong with that.

Having an opinion is healthy, but judging someone is not.

It really does not help anyone or anything or any situation if you talk badly about it. Think about it, you actually feel bad yourself for saying what you did. So, when you find yourself in a situation where you have nothing good to say about it, either say nothing or find something to be grateful for or something positive that is related to it.

I guess this is another example of "spreading your glitter."

Basically, "Mindful Speech" as it is now known, is a very healthy way to talk. It is worth stopping to think about what you are saying as it will affect the rest of your day, even longer. Obviously, if you are passionate about something and want to voice your opinion then it is ok to say what you think, and in some cases, this may be seen as being "not very nice" in someone else´s eyes. The secret to this advice is the art in understanding and being true to your own inner voice. If your own inner voice is giving you signals that what you are about to say is not nice, then it probably isn´t advisable to say it as it is not going to do you any good.

By learning to communicate mindfully, you will do yourself a huge favor and those around you will benefit too.

A smile costs nothing
but gives so much,
make sure to share yours ☺

We all know that feeling, you are in a queue or on a bus and suddenly someone smiles at you. It makes you feel nice and the natural reaction is to smile back. My Mam used to say it is the nicest way to share kindness without saying anything, just smile!

Some people don´t know how to smile because they carry a lot of sadness in them, others are worried, others too stressed to stop and smile. It is really important to share your smile to as many people as possible, it not only makes you feel good, it makes the person you are sharing your smile with feel good too.

My Mam would say:

"It costs nothing but it is worth millions,
it takes seconds but its effect can last forever,
it may be meaningless to you and it may mean the world to its receiver and it will never be wasted."

Apparently, according to scientists smiling releases endorphins that have many health benefits. So, by sharing a smile you are actually doing your own health good and making someone else´s day brighter. Some even say that smiling is a natural drug. It is free, makes you feel good and it is safe to get addicted to.

Treat others like you
want to be treated yourself

This was drummed into me like a broken record as I was a child, which I found particularly annoying at the time and I used to mock and laugh it off as Mam said it to me. However, if there is one quote, I am really grateful for, it is this one:

> *"Treat others like you yourself wish to be treated by them"*

This saying not only is the secret to my marriage, it is the secret to my success at work, my lovely friendships, my everyday life, my relationship with my neighbors, my colleagues, my friends even those people who I don´t really need in my life who sometimes get on my nerves, we all have a couple of them no don´t we? ☺ But most importantly and for which I am most grateful, this saying is the core of, and secret to, my happy family life. Now I am not saying we don´t have our ups and downs, of course we do. But it is exactly then that this saying kicks into action and supports me in the correct handling of it.

Using it with friends is the easiest form. I love my friends and I want them all to love me and love spending time with me, so I always try to give my best to them. I like to do things that make them happy, say things that make them feel good and share things that make us joyful. However, when things don´t go to plan and I find myself in a sticky situation, I always fall back to treating my friends how I myself, would like to be treated and although I sometimes get furious because my inner goddess is screaming at me to tell me they don't deserve me being nice to them or they deserve something else. If I treat them like I would like to be treated I feel good about myself and know I gave my best to the situation whatever the outcome.

When it comes to relationships, I think this is the secret to our happy marriage. My husband and I decided quite soon on in our relationship if it was going to work, we were going to have to be honest with our feelings, learn how to communicate respectfully and most importantly, we promised always to treat each other as we would treat our very best friends in all situations, including the heated discussions and disagreements. Over the years I have seen many relationships fail simply because the partners didn't communicate respectfully with each other. Often competing against each other and putting each other down to make themselves feel better. Blaming one another for their own lack of contentment, I am sure you get the picture. This doesn't happen when you treat your partner how you indeed would like to be treated. As you are now beginning to see, there are many advantages in following this advice.

The most important being:

"By measuring yourself on the behavior you offer, you will quickly find it is much easier to communicate."

It is ok to disagree, on the contrary it is really important to disagree and feel free to voice your opinion, and it is also important to allow your partner to disagree with you and have their own opinion.

What happens when you treat everybody as you would like to be treated, is that, what would otherwise have been an argument, suddenly turns into a healthy heated discussion, with no winners or losers, just two people accepting each other's point of view.

At work it allows you to keep your head up high and remain respected in your own eyes. Do not let yourself down by lowering yourself to someone else's level to argue with them. Always maintain your own moral high ground. This means respecting yourself in the discussion, it has been said that there are always 3 sides to every argument:

- Mine
- Yours
- The truth.

It takes a bigger person to walk away and or apologize than to stubbornly stand their ground. It is always up to you how your feel about situations which means sometimes you have to find room in your heart to forgive the bad and be grateful for the good. Don't expect others to make you happy, find happiness in making others happy and treat them how you want to be treated and then people will automatically treat you the same way back.

It is well known that people often respond to you the same way you respond to them or have you ever intensely disliked someone who loved you dearly? If you find it hard to treat someone nicely then you have to realign your feelings towards them, you have to learn how to activate a different part of them in you. The easiest way to do this, is to stop and think of reasons why you are grateful for this person, very quickly you will want to treat them with kindness and you will want them to treat you with same kindness and if you do so, you will see they are treating you kindly just like you are treating them kindly.

Sometimes we have to adapt, the best way to do so is to lead by example. Mam also said you can choose your friends but not your relatives and they are the hardest ones to please. If you keep this saying in mind you will always have nice relationships with people. Everyone has different characters and that's ok, on the contrary that's great. We don't have to be the same just accept others like you want to be accepted. Basically, Mam always said "just make the best of it" that means make the best of the relationship you can, the best of the conversation and then you automatically get the best version of the other person that is available to you. Either enjoy it or be nice and drift away still letting the person feel worthy and good just as you would like to be left feeling good yourself.

Mam always said:

"You cannot control whether or not someone else respects you, but you can control whether or not you respect yourself!"

By treating others how you yourself want to be treated means that you have offered your best. What comes back may not always be what you want and others may not grant you the same privilege. The secret is, that you will always walk away with your head up high knowing you offered your best.

Mam often said to me:

"Never, let yourself down by reducing yourself down to someone else´s level to win an argument. You win by staying true to yourself and by treating others with the same respect you would like to be treated with yourself! ☺ "

There are people in your life for a reason, a season and a lifetime.

Mam embraced the moment and the person she was sharing it with. She made everyone feel like they were her best friend and she made everyone feel they were very important to her, this wasn´t show, you really were the most important person at that moment. Mam had a real talent for this and for making people feel at ease in her company.

To Mam, it didn´t matter if you were her daughter or if you were standing next to her in the queue for the toilet, she embraced anyone who was in her life even if it was just with one of her beautiful smiles.

She always had a comment to make you feel good in her presence, it was the most natural thing in the world for her, she didn´t do it to get attention back, she did it to make **you** feel good.

She believed that people came into your life for reason and that they came at different times.

Some people for a specific reason, like being at a party together, sitting on the bus together etc. Others for a season like working together or sharing a hobby and being in a club together, even being neighbors and then people who you share your life with like your family, your best friends etc.

For Mam it was really important to make a difference, it didn´t matter why you were in her life, as long as she made a positive difference to you. Every day she tried to make a difference to the world around her.

She made the moment that you were in with her, feel good. It was a talent she had and it was something I am really grateful to have learnt from her. She would say to us:

"Be true to yourself
and
make a difference!"

You can make a difference by smiling, by saying something nice, by being kind, you can make a difference in so many ways and it will feel as good to you as it doesn't to the person you are making a difference to.

Don´t hold on to fear and don´t be afraid of change

"Don't let fear control you, you control fear!"

My Mam appeared to be so confident. She was as extrovert as she was introvert and she was brilliant at covering up her fear. She was never afraid to challenge a situation and sometimes she was painfully honest about things. (In fact in her latter years, I seriously used to wonder if she was missing a filter when it came to being truthful because she was often very honest in her approach to dealing with certain situations ☺)

Whenever change felt hard, she would always guide us in a really special way through it.

She would say to me:

Fi, feel your fear, what is it that you are scared of? Admit to it and move on, do it anyway even if you are scared. You don't know where your limits are until you have pushed past them, she always told me to go further than I thought I could and I would be pleasantly surprised.

I don't really like change if I am honest, I like things to stay as they are its comfortable, I guess most of us are like that but change has to happen it is necessary for us to progress in life and move forward, we didn't come to this earth just to stand still and stay in the same situation all our lives, we came to evolve, to experience things and to enjoy ourselves. Mam always said change brings new things and that in itself is good.

Insecurity and anxiety is in every single one of us and it is not a nice feeling. Some of us allow it to come out, some of us play over it, some of us give in to it and others attack it, whatever you do with anxiety and insecurity my Mam taught me to feel it and acknowledge it and then to find something that I am grateful for in my personality that will help me get through it.

An example of this was when I was 15 year old and I was going to a new school. I was terrified, not only had I been to an all girls convent and I was now about to join a mixed 6th form, I knew nobody at all. I was excited because I wanted this change, but that didn't take away the anxiety that was inside of me because I was scared. We sat outside in the car park and she said to me:

"Go and get it gorgeous, what are you most grateful to yourself for that can help you today?"

I answered:

"My smile!"

"Then go in there and knock their socks off with your smile!"

And off I went. I walked across the yard smiling and feeling confident, I probably looked stupid, but I felt strong. She helped me to replace my insecurity with something I knew I had that made me feel good. She helped me to realize, if I could like myself, I was half way there. She taught me to believe, if I had the power to feel insecure and anxious, I had a bigger power within me to overcome that feeling and to feel good again. She used to drive me mad because she normally followed by telling me it was "character building".

Today I am so grateful to her for helping me to form my character to a person I feel comfortable with, a person I am proud to be. Now as a grown woman I still have issues where I feel anxious and insecure, more so than ever since she has left us but she had set a seed inside of me to help me when that feeling of insecurity and anxiousness came, I had a greater feeling inside of me which would help me empower it and overcome the negative feelings and replace them with positive feelings.

The key to successful change is learning how to adapt to the change and that is what my Mam taught me so well. Change is necessary and good or bad it is always great because after change we experience something new and then things tend to work themselves out and when we look back what seemed and felt so bad, was actually a stepping stone to something great.
We have to have faith in change and we have to be in charge of our own minds. Change is healthy.

Just before I left her and I was going to do something new that I was anxious about she would say:

"You are braver
than you think
and stronger
than you feel
right now"

Change is always good because it is Character building!

You are the <u>best</u> person in this world, to be YOU

"By the grace of God
my darling,
you are
the best person
to be you"

This is such a comforting phrase that I have enjoyed hearing my whole life and one that I miss dearly. My Mams endless encouragement while I was growing up and as an adult, especially as a young mother, was amazing. She always found the right words to encourage me to follow my own instinct. This phrase was one that truly resonated with me.

We all know situations, relationships and experiences that we have, that make us feel insecure. I don´t think there is a human being on this planet that doesn´t doubt themselves at some point. When I reached this point, my Mam would discuss with me whatever it was I was feeling insecure about, then she would add: "Does it feel right to you?"

She wasn´t interested in the answer, she was interested in what I felt, if I was feeling true to myself through the actions that I was taking. She always told us not to change to please other people because we would never ever please them.

"It will never be enough!" she would say.
"Be yourself and it will work, don´t try to change to please others"

Mum always encouraged me to be empathetic towards other peoples feeling and opinions, but she always taught me to know who I was and to know where my boundaries were.

"You make you, nobody else, and by the grace of God you are the only and the best person that can possibly be you!"

"Stay unique
and don't change
for anyone
but you"

Everybody should have the courage to be themselves. I hope sincerely if nothing else in this book is of use to you, that you take these words and make them yours because my dear Mam also said regularly:

"This is no dress rehearsal!"

I love this because it is so true. We have this moment and this life and we all have to make the most out of what we have, we have to make it count….NOW!

Always show your appreciation
to others
and always say
"PLEASE & THANK YOU!"

This really is nothing special to most of us, as it is exactly how we have been brought up ourselves. But do you do it?

Saying PLEASE and THANK YOU is so important. It was drummed into me as a child and to most of my friends. As I grow older and I myself have become a mummy, I have realized just how valuable this advice is.

Saying please when you ask for something is so much more than just being polite. It is a sign of respect and kindness to the person you are requesting something from. There is so much more emotion in your request if you simply add "please" to it. Think about it yourself, if somebody asks you to do something and they don't say please, there is a small part of you that feels "put out" even "used". By simply adding "please" you automatically feel appreciated and most of the time you are actually happy to help.

By adding a "THANK YOU" to this you also leave the person who has done the gesture for you feeling happy and appreciated and much more likely to help you again in the future than if you just take it for granted that it was your right that they help you.

I actually live a bilingual life and in the culture that is second to me "please & thank you" are nowhere near as dominant in the language as in my first language and culture. This has led me to greatly appreciate the use of the words because I often miss the emotional gratitude and respect that the words give you when they are spoken.

So, next time to ask something of somebody, irrelevant of who they are, make sure you say "please & thank you" because you will make a real difference to the way the hear what you are saying to them and you will both have a much better day by showing this little gesture of kindness and respect to each other than by not doing it.

Use it consciously and I promise you, you will feel great yourself and the people you are communicating with will feel great communicating with you too.

On the beach of hesitation
lie the bones
of countless thousands
whom
while hesitating died

This was actually Mams´ interpretation of the famous quote from Adlai Stevenson:

"On the plains of hesitation lie the blackened bones of countless millions who at the dawn of victory lay down to rest, and in resting died."

Adlai Stevenson I

It was a saying she repeated time and time again. Mam was a doer, if she wanted something she wasn´t shy to go after it nor was she shy to work hard for it. What she never did was wait too long for the "right" time to come along. Mam truly believed that if you wait too long for something then you will miss your opportunity.

"There is no time like Now!"

She would say to us and she always encouraged us to move forwards and follow our dreams.

She encouraged us to follow what it was we wanted. To try and try again but never not to try. She would often say to us:

"If you wait for the right moment it will never come"

She was so right. During my life I have remembered this saying so many times to push me forwards and I am so grateful for all of the experiences I have had in doing so, some good, some not so good but all well worth it.

Kids need boundaries, unconditional love and space to develop

I have heard this said time and time again. Becoming a parent is one of the scariest and yet most fulfilling things that has ever happened to me. Your whole outlook on life changes. I remember asking my Mam as I was pregnant with my daughter whether or not she ever thought she ever doubted that she could be a parent. She laughed and told me she had regularly thought she couldn't do it, and it was in those times that she really noticed she was getting it right. She would tell me all the time:

*"All children need
are love,
boundaries
and
space to grow"*

As my daughter was born, she said that the biggest gift I could give my children was acceptance, it's the kindest and the hardest gift too she added.

I never really understood this properly until I had spent enough time watching my children grow up, as they developed their own personalities, I realized what she had meant. Sometimes as a parent you have to accept that your child may want to grow in a different way to the way that you would like them to grow, you have to give them room to experiment with their personalities. I guess what she meant was that as a parent it is our job to give our children clear boundaries, however to offer them enough space to grow into who they want to be and it is our job to love them unconditionally no matter whether it is what we think is best for them or not. It is so hard to love unconditionally, yet that is what we have to do, . We want so much for our children, we want them to be good at school, well behaved, we want them to be healthy, good in sport, well liked, good with people, good with animals, we want so much but what we have to do is allow them to develop how they want to develop. It´s like a caterpillar turning into a butterfly, we have to allow the cocoon to shed off bit by bit, because no matter what colour the butterfly is, it is always unique and beautiful in its own right and it is also very very fragile.

It is our job as parents, to cocoon the caterpillar and feed it with as much love as possible and then we have to wait and see how the butterfly comes out. That's what she told me about parenthood and in my eyes she did a perfect job and I can´t think of a better gift to give to your children than that, however as easy as it sounds it is so, so hard to do.

So all of you parents out there who are struggling either with toddlers or with teenagers or a 7 year old who think they are teenagers or with 22 year old who hasn´t yet realized they are no longer teenagers, the biggest gift you can give them space, acceptance and to thank god for the people they are and you will see what a wonderful, spectacular amazing beautiful person you have the joy of calling your child. And even as adults, young adults, older adults, they will always be your child and the most perfect version of them will always be the one you can dare to love unconditionally, hence their "true self."

Whatever you do,
do it gracefully

As I write this today, I have to think back over the generations of women in my family. Today would have marked the 116th birthday of one of my Nana's and the 100th birthday of my other Nana. I come from a long line of very strong women, but they have all had something else in common that I guess was the secret to their success, they were all very graceful women.

Don't get me wrong, gracefulness is not just to be enjoyed my women, on the contrary anyone can be graceful, it is a great attribute to have. It is just personally, I associate it as being a feminine trait whoever the owner is male or female.

My Mam always taught us, no matter what we do we should do it gracefully. I can remember being really small and asking her what she meant when she always told me to be graceful. Her answer has remained with me my entire life:

"it's simple pet,
whatever you do,
whoever you do it with,
always make it look easy,
do it with confidence,
speak highly of it or of them
and make it look attractive to all
who are watching you!"

In other words, I guess she was telling me to do things without complaining and to make the most of what I had without explaining myself to others and without making it look hard. Another word she used a lot was elegant. I guess being graceful means being elegant and being in control of both your actions and your feelings. More importantly my Mam meant that it was important to be graceful in order to show the person, thing or situation that you are interacting with, respect. "Never be aloof," she would say, "you are no better or worse than the man standing next to you if you treat each other with grace!"

Aiming to be graceful, (I say it like this because it isn't always easy to be graceful so all you can do is try your best!) has also helped me to deal with situations that are thrown at me that are hard. I always look for the "good" in situations and I truly believe that things will always work out for the best, no matter how rubbish the situation actually appears to be.

Being graceful allows me to be confident, because in order for me to act gracefully I have to be comfortable with myself. It is about uplifting those around me and seeing every moment and every person as being a special.

My Mam had a real talent of making anyone who had the pleasure of being in her company feel so special, it was a real gift and it was one of the things I heard so often from people after she had passed. I now know this was the "grace" she was trying to teach me her whole life.

It is definitely something that I have taken on board and I think this was one of the nicest pieces of advice I was given as I was growing up and one that I definitely share with my world regularly, whoever they may be. I also gain much more pleasure out of situations by reacting to them gracefully, I guess it makes my life easier too.

Failure leads to expansion

Most of us are brought up believing that failure is a bad thing. Not me!

I was taught that failure is a good thing because it gives me the chance to grow. My Mam would always say:

"Don't worry
it is
character building!"

Sometimes my brother, sister and I would scream at her saying:

"I don't need my character building up anymore, I am happy with who I am!"

She would smile and reply:

"That's not your choice!"

As a middle-aged woman I actually still tell myself when things challenge me that I don't need to worry it is character building and it actually feels quite soothing, at least it makes me smile.

I was also taught from a very young age not to ponder too long on failure but instead to look for the opportunities to be gained from failure and to act on them. Whether it was a Latin vocabulary test or a lost game of netball, my Mam would turn the failure around to find something positive that would eventually lead to expansion and to success. I have to admit this is something I miss so much not that she has passed. We literally talked 2 or 3 times every day, the smallest challenge that I faced in a day I loved to call her and hear her point of view, she just had an amazing perception of being able to find the good in things.

Mam taught us, admittedly a lot through sport which was a passion we shared together, that failure could sometimes be more valuable that success. When we lost a game, she immediately went into lessons learned, she focused firstly on what we did right, then on where we could have done better. She NEVER said we had got it wrong, instead she said we learnt one way not to do it next time.

As I have grown up and older I have realized what it was that my Mam was doing. When we faced failure, she didn´t make excuses like a lot of people do as to why we should have got it right and that it wasn´t our fault etc. No, she faced it head on, she accepted it had gone differently to expected but instead of looking for excuses she looked for things that I personally could change to make it work next time. It often reached the point that I got excited to try again, this time I felt armed and in control to succeed. To this day, I never spend a lot of time crying over spilt milk, I move on swiftly and gracefully ready to embrace the next challenge.

I think the message here is simply, I am not afraid to fail because I was taught there is good to be found in failure and so I don´t fear failure.

Never Judge!

Don't judge! just be the best version of yourself you can be and let others be the best version of themselves that they can be and you won't go wrong.

You can allow others to judge you, but you don't have to care about pleasing them or what their opinion is because you always have a choice as to whether or not you let them get to you. It is not your job to make people feel good by being perfect for them, people have to find a way to feel good themselves and to find you perfect, just because you are YOU.

We have to allow each other to have our own preferences and to allow each other to evaluate situations, but we don't have to judge others nor do we have to allow others to judge us. It is OK to compare ourselves to each other, but it's not ok to judge which is better, because it depends on the perspective, we look at it and we can only decide or judge on what is right for us from our point of view, we can never judge for someone else. We simply have to be unconditional with each other.

Like most teenagers, sometimes growing up I would feel misunderstood from my peers or I may have fallen out with one of my friends because some nasty words had been shared. My Mam was always great, she would say to me:

"If someone takes the time
to examine you,
see it as a compliment,
but don't let them
get inside of you."

I treasure this advice to this very day. You cannot help someone else´s jealousy or misunderstanding of you, you really have to accept that. But you can definitely help whether or not you allow their misunderstanding of you and their opinion or judgement of you to get to you. You have to take a step back, allow them their opinion, they can only judge you if you allow them to. If their opinion doesn´t matter then it can´t judge you.

This advice is really valuable but very hard to live. It is definitely one of the things Mam talked about that I still battle with on a daily basis, because sometimes, in fact a lot of the time, other people´s opinions do count for me. I guess we all want to be accepted and told we are doing ok and this is where the advice gets really important:

*"You have to be enough to yourself
and your own opinion
of yourself
has to be worth more to you
than anyone else´s,
you will never please others
if you can´t
please yourself!"*

"On top of this, you are allowed to have an opinion on someone or something, that´s for you personally. What you are not allowed to do, is to allow that opinion to turn into judgement, everyone has their reasons for being who they are and doing what they do, just as you have your reasons for being who you are and doing what you do, your job is to accept it in a way that works for you, not to expect someone else to change to meet your approval!"

Give freely
and
receive gracefully

My Mam was a born giver. Whether it was a gift, a cake she baked for her neighbor or her time. My Mam got at least as much pleasure, if not more pleasure from giving than she did from receiving.

She would say:

*"We don't give to get
and sometimes
you will receive in return
from a very different place
than from where you gave to."*

She encouraged us always to give freely without expecting in return. This was the easy part, if you are a "giver" and we are in my family then giving is a pleasure and you get great comfort from doing so. It simply delights you to see the pleasure someone else gets from what you have to give to them.

The hard part is receiving. As Mam used to tell us "you don't give to get!" neither should you feel obliged "to give because you got!"

When you give it should be done from your heart freely and unconditionally. When you receive it should be with grace, appreciation and humility.

I love this saying so much and I get great pleasure in both giving freely and gracefully receiving so much so that it actually enhances the pleasure of both giving and receiving even more.

There is good in everything and everyone

"It's everywhere and in everything, you just have to look for it!"

Sometimes we find ourselves in some dark places and believe me I know these too. It is of no fault of our own, life sometimes just deals us a hard set of cards. Mam never taught us to avoid accepting that a situation was grim or bad, but she did teach us that nothing was dark enough to not be able to find light in it and nothing was bad enough for there not to be good found in it somewhere.

"There is no darkness that isn't hiding light. It doesn't matter how hard times get sweetheart, always look for the good, you always have a reason to be grateful and that will help change things for the better."

This advice means that when I find myself in a situation that quite literally feels awful, I stop and reassess, I look again and again until I find the light, even if it is a tiny thing.

Take the way my Mam left this earth as an example.

It was most definitely the worst thing that has ever happened to me. I was filled with excitement standing at the airport waiting for my dear Mam to come through the gates and she didn't arrive.

My excitement changed to despair in the blink of an eyelid. If someone had told me this was going to happen, I would have sworn I couldn't cope with it, but I did. I was faced with my Mam on a life support machine with initially no chance of survival. I could have fallen into despair, given up, asked Why me? (Mam would have immediately replied "why not you?") I could have collapsed into a heap but I didn't, admittedly I was not full of joy, I was desperately sad, I was lost in the sadness I was experiencing.

I didn't get out of this situation alone, I was lucky enough to have my brother and sister with me who shared the same upbringing.

Together we carried each other, we quoted our mother, we asked ourselves what would she do? We found reasons to laugh with her lying unconscious in her ICU bed, we spoke words of gratitude and we found comfort in the fact that she was giving us time to get used to knowing that she was going to leave us.

When she closed her eyes to walk over the rainbow 5 weeks later, we walked out of the hospital and the first thig we said to each other was:

"we were so lucky to have had her!"

Those words say it all. In the darkest hole you can find light if you look hard enough and it is normally in the form of gratitude.

If you struggle with a person who is getting to you. Mam would normally say:

"Bless them and send them on their way!"

Meaning forgive them for whatever it is that is bothering you and move on without them.

If you still struggle then the advice, she gave was simple;

Find something to be grateful about
even if it is
as simple as knowing
that you want nothing to do
with them.
Thank them, for showing you, the
person you no longer
want, to allow to hurt you
and move on.

The more you can find to be grateful for, the easier it
will be to forgive and in forgiveness we can all move
forward.

It is grudge and lack of forgiveness that ties us down,
forgiveness and gratitude will set you free.

Mam believed that there was a plus and minus
everywhere. She never denied that it was hard to find,
sometimes it is like looking for a needle in a haystack,
but she believed that if you look hard enough you will
find it.

Mam would say:

*"If it looks bad,
look harder
to find
the good."*

Growing up people would often say to me; "it's easy for you Fi, if you fall in shit you will come out smelling of roses!" But that's not always true. The truth is, Mam taught me that if I fall in shit like everyone else does, while I am in it, I don't look for the shit I look for the roses, I look for the sweet smell of roses somewhere and eventually I will find something very small, often insignificant to most, but I will find something that I am grateful for and I concentrate on it and slowly the shit starts smelling of roses.

That is quite simply how I live my life. I look for the smell of roses in shit and find it!

(So sorry for using the word Mam ☺)

Share your magic
and
embrace the moment

"Yesterday is history,
tomorrow is a mystery,
today is a gift
so, live it
to the best
of your ability!"

My Mam loved this saying. She taught us this lesson later in life, I guess as she herself was learning it. We were so lucky, these days it is quite trendy to live in the moment and all of us have heard it said to us. My Mam went a step further, she would say to us:

"This is no dress rehearsal so, give your best!"

This is so true. We really do not have any more than the moment we are living in, so be mindful about how you live it. Accept what was, gracefully and look forward with excitement to what may come, but always take the time to be grateful for what it is that your moment is offering you and enjoy it because that is all you have right now!

If you give your best and share the best you have to offer (Mam called this your magic!) then you can be at ease knowing that you did the best you could and as she so often told us:

*"we can't ask more
than that
of you!"*

Inferiority
is easily overcome,
use superiority
and make
people feel good.

"Make people
feel good
it´s contagious"

This has been such great advice in many different situations in my life. I use it at work, at home, with friends and even simply out and about at the shops and parking my car. It actually makes my world a much nicer place to be.

We can´t all be perfect for each other and there are definitely some of us who feel they are better than others and there are most certainly plenty of us who feel we are less worthy than others. For whatever reason this may be, be it right or wrong, my Mam armed me with a mindset that easily and swiftly allows me to overcome all of the anxiety and unease that an inferiority complex brings with it.

There is simply no explanation as to why some people feel that it is their right to feel better than others. To be honest my personal opinion on this is that it is because they don´t feel happy within themselves so they rely on others to make them feel good. Whatever the reason it really doesn´t matter because I certainly cannot solve that problem for them, only they can learn to love themselves and be "enough" just by being "them!"

However, these people cause the rest of us regular heartache because when they aren´t "enough" to themselves, they rely on us to make them feel good.

This generally happens by them putting us down and making us feel "inferior" to them in order to allow them to feel "superior" to us.

Mam had a simple and easy way of dealing with this:

"Get in first, make them feel good!"

This meant, giving them a compliment, say something to make them feel good and they won't knock you down. It is so simple and it works every time. The best thing is, it costs you nothing and actually its quite nice to make someone feel good in fact it is contagious, you will see it will catch on.

I will give you an example.

We had a neighbor who thought she was the queen of the street, I have no idea where she got this from or what made her think she was king pin, it really doesn't matter she did and that was that. She would knock on our door and walk in the house and before saying hello she would say, there was a funny smell or ask if there was something new, it looked funny, whatever it was she would knock our house. She didn't do this consciously and she wasn't being horrid (although there are people who do this consciously and this trick works with them too) she simply came to our house to make herself feel better. She would then proceed to tell my Mam what she had done that was better and then leave feeling so much better because she had found someone to feel inferior to her because our house smelt and hers didn't. (I know this sounds bizarre but it's a simple example to help make the mindset clear) Mam changed her tactic, when she saw our neighbor come, she didn't as you would think spray an air freshener, no that would have just fueled her fire even more and made her feel even more superior and Mam more inferior. No, Mam opened the door and before the neighbor could say anything she said: "You look lovely today, have you been to the hairdressers?" She felt good before she crossed the door, she then came in and was normal, Mam made her feel good, that was after all what she was coming for, not to knock Mam, in fact it had nothing to do with Mam it was entirely to do with the neighbor. Mam made her feel superior without feeling inferior herself, on the contrary she felt indifferent to her.

It really costs nothing to make people feel good, so next time you feel put down by someone, widen your mindset and ask yourself what you can do to help them feel better. It is not about you if someone is knocking you down and making you feel inferior it is ALWAYS about THEM. So, help them on their way and make them feel good. Believe me it will make your day brighter too.

If you are a Duchess, then be a Duchess

When I was born my family nicknamed me "the Duchess."

It was mainly because of the way I conducted myself from the day I was born. Admittedly I was the youngest and the age gap between me and my brother and sister is quite a lot so I guess I was the "little one" of the family and I guess I regularly used that to my advantage ☺

One day I was really disappointed by the way someone at school had been treating me and I really didn´t understand why she was doing so. I had done nothing to her, the circumstance for which she was picking on me for were beyond my control (my parents were getting divorced and as a good catholic family this was seen by some as inacceptable, but it certainly wasn´t my doing nor could I do anything about it).

Mam asked me what was wrong and I told her, her reply to me stayed with me forever:

"are you our Duchess?" she asked
"Yes" I replied

"Then why do you allow others to treat you as if you weren´t? How dare someone assume they know about your home life or the situation they are picking on you for without having ever been inside of our house.

You are our Duchess and I will give you some advice.

"If you want to be treated like a
Duchess then
either be with people
who treat you like one
or
treat yourself like one
and remove yourself
from the situation
that is making you
not feel like a Duchess,
*but **<u>don´t not</u>** be a Duchess!"*

It is a shame
to be shabby!

I love this one. I am a Geordie and I was brought up in Newcastle in the North East of England and we heard this saying all the time. It always puts a smile on my face because it does two things with me.

Firstly, and most importantly it confirms to me that it is OK to spoil myself and have something nice. Secondly, it reminds me where I come from and that always makes me so proud.

Shabby means that someone or something is not very well cared for and the saying "it´s a shame not to do something" means that it is sad not to do something, it would be a waste if you didn´t do it.

This saying implies that it is a shame not to dress nicely or treat yourself to something new, something "chic" that is perhaps a little bit extravagant. In Geordie terms: It is a shame not to be lush ☺

The saying "it´s a shame to be shabby!" basically means, well done you for being worth it to yourself and treating yourself to something lovely, often a little bit extravagant or something that appears extravagant. It is not about being expensive it is about the impression it makes and how it boosts you. It is about being good to yourself.

Mam you were so right, it really is a shame to be shabby!

Bless them
and
send them
on their way

Forgiveness was such a huge part of my Mams life. She didn't suffer fools easily on the contrary to be honest you didn't mess with my Mam. If she felt wrongly done to by you, boy did she let you know it. However, what she taught me was that it is OK to be hurt, it is OK to be annoyed and it is OK to need space to sort an issue out.

It is however not OK to hold a grudge, nor is it OK to assume you are right and the other person is wrong. She taught us, when there is no solution and no way of agreeing on a matter then it is time to forgive.

She practiced this from small incidents like not getting annoyed with someone pushing in a queue in front of her, to big rifts. She would pray for forgiveness and for help to be shown how to give the person she had fallen out with or got annoyed with, forgiveness.

She accepted that the other person didn't understand her point of view and that she couldn't, for whatever reason, understand their point of view.

This by no means meant that she agreed with the other person, there was no way my mother ever backed down when she thought she was right. What she did do, and what she taught us to do, was to learn to draw a line, learn to know when it has gone too far and learn to know when it was hurting her more to try and prove her point that it would be, to forgive them.

It is really important here to understand forgiving someone in her eyes was not the same as giving in to them, no that was far from what she was doing. What she was doing was protecting herself, when the matter in question was getting out of hand. She chose her battles wisely, she didn't suffer unnecessarily and when she saw she was not going to win, she would turn the situation around and stop it in its tracks.

Although this often hurt her emotionally, she still always tried to forgive them. She would say:

"I can forgive you,
but I cannot forget
what you did yet
because I still do not understand it,
time will have to heal that!"

In so many ways I often think my Mam was born without a filter for certain situations. She said, especially in her later years, exactly what she was thinking. She was sometimes painfully truthful. This has been one of the hardest things for me to understand from the morals she taught me. She would always say:

"Honesty is
the best policy!"

If you know what you are dealing with, and you can only decide this for yourself, then you can offer forgiveness.

I guess the secret behind this wisdom is simply, be honest and be ready to forgive because there is always another version to everything and if you cannot see that then don´t hurt yourself by feeling hurt by someone else´s behavior.

You don't always know their motivation. Sometimes we have to agree to disagree and move on. Simply put:

"Bless them
and send them
on their way!"

It is how
you feel
that matters

My Mam always taught us to listen to our instinct. I remember on many occasions in my life when I needed to make a decision my Mam would say 2 things:

Don´t be afraid of change!

How does your decision make you feel?

And then came the secret, she added:

Really feel? Be honest!

Over time I have learned to live my life according to this principle. I use it for absolutely everything from really important decisions like moving house, investing money, career moves to choosing what I want to eat when we are out for dinner, or even which book to read before I go to sleep at night.

It is actually a lot of fun, it´s like a game. Mam did always say this earth was a play-ground for us to have as much fun as possible in. Start playing this "feeling game" to make easy decisions.

Take for example it is Saturday afternoon and you are in town and you decide you want to go for a coffee. Take a moment to stop and think, Where do I want to go? Which feels better coffee shop A or coffee shop B? This may feel strange at first but once you start getting in touch with your inner voice helping you to be in touch with how you truly feel, you will see how richer your life becomes. The secret behind this is in being able to choose always to feel good, we start to live more easily, we are behind our decisions because we make them consciously, we generally choose the one that feels good, if it turns out otherwise it doesn´t matter we can make a new decision to change it. The most important thing is YOU are making your decisions, you aren´t making them to make someone else feel good, you are in touch with your own feelings. This is really important because Mam also taught me, you will never make anyone else truly happy, they have to do that themselves. You can make yourself happy and that´s it, and in order to do that you have to be in touch with the way you feel every minute of every day in every situation wherever it may be and whoever it may be with.

A very important point she made was never to feel shame for who you are or who you want to become, this is your life and as long as you feel good about yourself do not let others allow you to feel shame. You choose how you feel, NOT them!

Have fun playing ☺

**If you say you can you can
If you say you can´t you can´t!**

I have cursed at these words so many times in my life that I have lost count how many times it was. Growing up I was always a very inquisitive, alert little girl but there was one thing I always relied on, that was, knowing that I was confident simply knowing my Mam was always behind me.

These words were instilled into my DNA. If ever, and belief me once I learned the power of these words it wasn't that often, I said I can't, my Mam immediately said:

*"If you say you can
you can!
If you say you can't
you can't!"*

These words are really powerful. It really is true that if we believe in ourselves then we are far more lightly to achieve than if we assume, we cannot succeed.

Even now as an adult, and my friends who do exercise classes with me will confirm this, I find myself saying:

"Fi you can, Fi you have got this, come on Fi you can!"

It's like a little encouragement angel that abides within my head. I push myself because I believe I can, I never stop myself because I believe I can't and there within lies the secret.

If you ask the questions, listen to the answer

We all know this, we ask and we ask but do we actually listen to the answer we are being given. Sometimes when things aren´t going how we want them to we often get very inquisitive in asking questions, especially the "why" question.

"Why is it going like that?"
"Why did he say that?"
"Why did she act like that?"

My Mam often stopped me when I was doing this and she would say to be:

"Be careful what you are asking if you don´t stop and listen to the answer!"

This was such good advice. So next time you ask a question listen to the answer before you ask the next one! Just because it is not what you want to hear doesn´t mean it´s not an answer. You have to re-align and act on what you have, change the question or act on the answer.

Life is cruel
for taking away our loved ones,
but kind
for giving them to us
in the first place

Loosing someone is always really hard. Sadly 2 years before my Mam left us we lost our dear Dad to cancer. Although my parents were divorced and had been for most of my life, they were the best of friends. They had a friendship that was mainly due to the fact that they had 3 kids together and 4 grandchildren and both of them loved their respective roles as Mam, Grandma, Dad and Grandad.

My Dad died in my arms and it was my first direct contact with death. I was not prepared for it nor did we expect it to come in the moment it did, but it did and I dealt with it as well as I possibly could. It felt very peaceful to me and I remember for weeks after repeating the same sentence:

"I don´t know where Dad went but he certainly didn´t die, it was just his body that gave up!"

I struggled after this experience and my Mam helped me through the hard days, weeks and months that followed.

A couple of days after his funeral I was lying on her sofa, it was Christmas and I had 2 little kids that I was supposed to preparing Christmas for, it didn´t matter what I did I just couldn´t help myself. I said to her:

"Mam, you taught me there is good in everything, where is the good in this?"

Her reply was:

"Nobody can take away the pain
of death
but you yourself
can turn it around,
for we die on one single day of our
lives, all of the others we lived
and
we shared some amazing times
and experiences together,
they are the ones
that we should be remembering
and not the day
someone dies."

I thought about this for a long time and then I started to think about all of the lovely times we had shared together, all of the things I loved about my Dad, all of the traits I had inherited from him good and bad, but they were ours, things we shared together and nobody or nothing could take those from me. Mam was right, the memories were what I should be thinking about because they made me feel better, they made me smile, they filled me with gratitude, they eased the pain.

Mam added:

"If it hurts so much to lose someone
then it must have been good
while it lasted
and you most certainly
have more reasons
to be happy
than to be sad."

She was so right.

I couldn't change the fact that Dad had gone, I couldn't
ignore the pain and emptiness that I was feeling inside,
but I could change the way I was viewing it, I could
think of the good times and I could be grateful for what I
had.

As I continued to do this over the following weeks, the
pain didn't get easier but it became bearable and it was
actually comforting to sit down and remember Dad and
the great times we had instead of reminding myself he
was gone.

Don´t hate
just intensely dislike

This is clear in its statement but is it as clear in the understanding of it?

The reason my Mam told us not to "hate" be it things or people, was not because of the recipient but because of the way it made you yourself feel.

Mam would say:

"Hate has as much power
as love
only in the wrong direction."

Not liking something is normal. It is ok and everyone is entitled to their own opinion. On the contrary it is really healthy to always know who you are and what you want and how you feel about something or someone.

However, "hating" someone or something does something very different to you. Fell the emotion of it. Just stop and think about it.

How do you feel when you say:

"I hate that!"

As opposed to :

"I don't like that?"

Can you feel the difference? Well that is what she meant.

The feeling of "hate" generates a really awkward feeling within you. The feeling of "hate" is much more intense than that of "dislike," this leads to your brain processing the information you are feeling differently.

Hate initiates much more anger than dislike does.

Take the time to check yourself and next time you go to use the word "hate" think twice and use "dislike" instead. I promise you, you will feel so much better for doing so!

If you fall in shit, make sure you come out smelling of roses

I love this one. It epitomizes my dear mam and her never ending optimism and love for life. As you have read in many chapters of this book, my dear mam was a very optimistic and life-loving individual. There wasn´t much phased her but nearly everything inspired her, nothing more so than a challenge.

If ever we found ourselves in a bit of a mess, this was her favorite saying:

"If you fall in shit,
don´t worry about what you have
fallen in, just make sure
you come out smelling of roses!
It is after all
how you rise again
that will determine
whether the fall
was worth it or not!"

She taught us that we couldn´t get things wrong, that every experience we had was character building and that if we learnt by our so-called mistakes then they weren´t mistakes because in fact everything we do in this life is for a reason so there is good in everything as long as we look hard enough to find it.

This was never so true as when we really did find ourselves in the xxxx.

What she actually meant with this saying was not that we cover up the mess we have found ourselves in by covering ourselves in roses, as the saying may suggest when you first read it but instead she meant we had to make the most of the situation we were in however bad it may seem and turn it around to find something good in it. The "smelling of roses" was making the best out of a bad situation.

Let me give you an example:

When I got my first job I was a really ambitious young lady, I honestly believed, thanks to my amazing upbringing, that the world was at my feet. I had high ambitions and was ready to conquer the world. I was particularly aware of my strengths as a woman, especially as I was working in the engineering trade and I was quite exotic as a woman, in fact I was the first and only woman in our sales department. One day I got asked if I would like to apply for the job as the assistant to the managing director, well I was so happy and of course I did it. Unfortunately, I didn´t get the job and I was gutted. I called my Mam and in my mind it was everybody else´s fault that I didn´t get the job and in my mind they hadn´t seen me or given me a fair interview, I think you get the picture, I had fallen into shit! Her response was calm and cool:

"Wow pet, you did your best. What a great experience that was, meeting the managing director and getting the chance to have an interview with him. What did you learn from that?"

My response:

"Mam you aren´t listening, I didn´t get the job, it was all a waste of time, all of that effort and preparation for nothing. I am gutted!"

Mam´s response:

"Fi, how do you know that you went through that to get the job? Perhaps there was another reason for you doing it, now answer my questions, what did you learn from it?"

Of course I gave a million answers why I was annoyed and how unfair it had been and if I had only been given another chance it may have been different, until she asked me:

"What do you know now, that you didn´t know before?"

My reply:

"I know I was good enough but I wasn´t what he wanted, we didn´t match!"

Mam

"well that smells like roses!"

….by the time we had finished I was no longer sad that I hadn´t been given the opportunity to take the job because my Mam had changed my mindset around to take the best out of the situation I had in hand and not to dwell on what I couldn´t have. She taught me to keep looking until I found something that felt right.

The secret here was in the "feeling ok", it is essential no matter what we do in life and how bad things appear, to find something that "feels ok" and then build on that. That is the secret to falling into shit and coming out smelling of roses!

As it happened my life took a huge turn around not long afterwards and I would never have been able to pull the job off as it would have been far too stressful and far too much travelling and it would never have worked out with the changes that came shortly afterwards. And those changes really were life-changing and superb for me and I still smile now when I think how good it was that I didn't get that job ☺ OMG she was right again!

Happiness is an inside job!

Talk about saving the best for last. If you take nothing else from this book please take this with you. It was my Mam´s most used saying, yet something she battled with her whole life.

Happiness
really is
an inside job!

We all want to be happy. It is a blissful state of mind that is like no other feeling, the feeling of contentment is magical. However, we all tend to stand in our own way to happiness because for some reason form the day we are born to tend to rely on others to provide us with happiness instead of looking within.

It will give you so much freedom if you can start to live your life believing this truth. Mam was brought up differently to us and in times where it did matter, apparently! What others thought. So it was by no means natural to her or probably to anyone from her generation to believe that you yourself are responsible for your own happiness. It was something that life taught her and that she was determined to give to me. She would often say:

"Learn from my mistakes,
don´t give anyone
that freedom to control your
happiness,
it is so precious,
it´s yours,

treasure it pet."

Your rules decide what makes you happy nobody elses
and you have to pave the way to your own happiness.
Mam always encouraged us to be good to ourselves, she
would often say to me:

"don't beat yourself up pet,
you did your best."

She would say to me that it was about making my
experience pleasing for me, and that doesn't mean you
are selfish, on the contrary, if you are happy people
around you tend to be happy too. It is part of our
happiness knowing that we have made others happy and
if you can get there it is a really awesome feeling. It is
about changing your perception to suit you, find an angle
that makes you happy and don't rely on others to show
you the way. Nobody can ever really know what
happiness means to you, they can offer you kind gestures
that add to your perception of happiness, but in the end it
the feeling you experience that decided whether or not
you are happy and nobody except you can feel that.

Wherever you find yourself, find something in it that
makes you happy and build from there. And never
forget:

"It's YOUR happiness, treasure it!"

She also added to this:

"And because happiness is an inside
job, never forget
that the greatest gift
you can give another person
is the space to be themselves
and to find
their own happiness!"

To sum it up!

I have no doubt that most of you who have read this book have regularly found things in it that reminded you in some way of your own experiences. This is because a mother's love is unconditional. There is not a mother on this planet who does not in some way feel it is their job to give guidance to their child. Even if the circumstances around some women who give birth are not ideal, I firmly believe each and every mother feels unconditional love and this in turn leads to wanting the best for your child even if it isn't always possible to give it.

My dear Mam was right about so many things, she was so lucky to find her passing in the way it was. She left this earth on her way to her Granddaughters birthday, dressed in her favorite designer label, with her nails painted gold. She had joy in her soul and love and excitement in her heart.

You may be asking yourselves:

"What was lucky about that, she didn't make it to the party?"

The fact is, as she so regularly said "when you time is up, it's up and there is no jumping or skipping the queue!"…………Mam would answer that question by saying;

"the answer to that question lies within"

And guess what?
you were right every time!

Life doesn´t always deal us the best of cards nor is it
always easy, but hey there´s one I forgot:

My dear Mam always said:

*"nobody said
it would be easy Pet!"*.

And on that note:

Thanks Mam

xxx

Who was Pat?

Patricia Mary Bernadette Haylock, as she liked to be called on Sundays, was born on the 25th March 1943 in York in the North of England. She was one of three children and she sadly faced her first tragedy at the young age of 5 when her father suddenly passed away with an aneurism. One of her memories and the reason for her tremendous faith was the belief that the "Lord" himself came to the house to lead the funeral procession, it wasn't until years later she realized that the gentlemen who led the precession that morning was indeed by status a "Lord" of the land and not "The Lord" from heaven, as she so had naively believed for years.

It was this belief that helped her as a very young girl through the hard years that followed. Her mother widowed with 3 young children just after the war, like many, they lived through hard times. Pat's happy, optimistic and cheerful nature carried her through the days, all she secretly wished for was a new Daddy. Her wish was granted at the age of 10 when her mother remarried an army officer who adoringly took on all three children and brought them up as his own. Jack had a huge influence on Pat's life, he was a man of few words, but of wise words.

Their life together took them overseas to West Africa, another huge influence on Pat's life. It was here she developed her empathy and passion for each and every individual that crossed her path. It never made a difference who you were to Pat, she treated everybody the same, she made everybody feel like for the moment you were with her, **you** were THE most important person in her life, and indeed this is how she has been remembered by many. This was one of her many attributes.

In her teenage years she and her family returned to the UK and settled in Newcastle Upon Tyne. It was here she met her first husband, "the nice man from over the road!". Pat and David were happily married for many years, they had 3 children together whom they both adored and they remained close friends their whole lives although they divorced after 21 years of marriage. Pat was a dedicated mother who wanted so much for her children, most of all she strived to maintain an environment filled with love, security and opportunity, she taught her children life skills, the skill to take life "Head on" as she would say. She gave her children wings and they all flew from the nest. They flew with wisdom and advice that they would only learn to treasure much later on in life.

As a grandmother Pat continued to share her wisdom, she always had time, she was never too busy and nothing was more important if she was needed by her family. In her capacity as a professional, Pat enjoyed a successful career where she was awarded for many achievements least of all being the Top Sales Woman for Royal Life Insurance in 1988. This was a true achievement she believed very much in the power of women and in fair emancipation.

However, her true passion apart from her family was sport. From a very young age, Pat was a very successful netball player. In her sporting career she attained 2 county blazers, one for netball and one later in life as a county bowler and her highest achievement was to become an All England Umpire for which she was awarded the England Blazer.

Pat loved that competitive edge, she only ever compared herself to herself but she believed in herself enough to push herself to the limits that she believed she could go to. Her wisdom, her advice and her approach to life were indeed her secret to success. She never gave up.

Pat was for her family:

A Guardian Angel
Their very best friend
And their life-long teacher

She devoted her whole life to ensuring her family, her friends, her colleagues in fact anyone whose life she touched, aspired and was encouraged to be the very best they possibly could be.

Pat was an extremely smart woman, ready for any occasion.

Her greatest quality was to '**ENCOURAGE**' - she believed there was no obstacle that   could not be overcome.

Through her life´s teachings we now understand:

"Love is unconditional
and
humble self-belief is the secret"

It is with pride I find myself sharing this knowledge with you all in this book and as I finish, I can proudly say:

Oh My God

my Mother was right!

The End.

Printed in Great Britain
by Amazon